Executive Producers: **Kim Mitzo Thompson, Karen Mitzo Hilderbrand**
Music Arranged By: **Hal Wright**
Music Vocals: **The Nashville Kids Sound**
Illustrated By: **Sharon Lane Holm**
Book Design: **Jennifer Birchler**

Published By:
Twin Sisters Productions
4710 Hudson Drive
Stow, OH 44224 USA
www.twinsisters.com   1-800-248-8946

©℗2010 Twin Sisters IP, LLC
All Rights Reserved. Made in China.

Read- and Sing-Along is a registered trademark of Twin Sisters IP, LLC.

ISBN-13: 978-159922-495-4

Jesus loves the little children,
All the children of the world.

Red, brown, yellow, black and white,
They are precious in His sight.
Jesus loves the little children of the world.

Jesus died for all the children,
All the children of the world.

Red, brown, yellow, black and white,
They are precious in His sight.
Jesus died for all the children of the world.

Jesus loves the little children,
All the children of the world.

Red, brown, yellow, black and white,
They are precious in His sight.
Jesus loves the little children of the world.

Jesus loves me, this I know,
For the Bible tells me so!

Little ones to Him belong.
They are weak but He is strong.

Yes, **Jesus** loves me!
Yes, **Jesus** loves me!

Yes, Jesus loves me,
The Bible tells me so!

Jesus, take this heart of mine.
Make it pure and wholly Thine.

On the cross You died for me.
I will try to live for Thee.

Yes, **Jesus** loves me!
Yes, **Jesus** loves me!
Yes, **Jesus** loves me,
The Bible tells me so!

Yes, **Jesus** loves me!
Yes, **Jesus** loves me!
Yes, **Jesus** loves me,
The Bible tells me so!
The Bible tells me so!